Echoes of Environmental Justice

Poetry and Prose

Dr. Kwaku Kusi-Appiah

TI: Echoes of Environmental Justice: Poetry and Prose
AU: Kwaku Kusi-Appiah

Front cover and interior images: Paintings by Laurence Phiri of Malawi

The best efforts have been made to respect copyright holders as well as people and organizations mentioned in the work. Should you have any comments, please contact the author at AndyKusiAppiah@cunet.carleton.ca

Softcover 978-1-998321-48-3

5.5" x 8.5"
Arial 9
Times New Roman 11 / 12
ca. 8,000 words
70 lb paper
60 pages

Copyright © Kwaku Kusi-Appiah 2025

Petra Books 2025
petrabooks.ca

Echoes of Environmental Justice

Painting by Laurence Phiri

Echoes of Environmental Justice

Forward

The delicate and powerful connections between humanity, nature, and justice are woven together with both urgency and hope. Each poem presents a call to action — an invitation to reflect on our relationship with the earth, to confront the injustices that harm both our environment and the communities that depend on it, and to recognize the sacred responsibility we all share in shaping a more sustainable and equitable future.

These poems touch on the aftermath of colonialism, environmental degradation, gender inequalities, and the complex forces of exploitation that continue to mar our world. Yet they also embody resilience—the resilience of nature, of Indigenous knowledge, and of people fighting for justice. From the rhythms of water and the whispers of nature's voice to the struggles for accessible spaces and the quest for a more just world, these poems remind us that our destiny is interwoven with the Earth's fate.

Whether addressing the political climate at COP29[1], the struggle for water and resources, or the pursuit of equality and environmental justice, the poems in this collection beckon us to pause, listen, and rise to the challenge. The future is not a distant place but rather one that is created in each moment, through our collective actions and a shared commitment to both people and planet.

---

[1] COP29, an abbreviation for the 29th Conference of the Parties to the United Nations Framework Convention on Climate Change (UNFCCC) held in Baku, Azerbaijan from November 11–22, 2024.

As you read, you may be inspired to consider how your own actions ripple through the fabric of life, and how we might, together, create a world where justice, equity, and sustainability are not just ideals, but lived realities for all.

> Dr. Andy Kwaku Kusi-Appiah (aka Kwaku Twum)
> Political Ecologist & Environmental Philosopher

Acknowledgments / Dedication

To the guiding spirit of wisdom and love, whose steady hand shaped my earliest memories and nurtured my connection to the land, Akua Akrasi[2], you have been a beacon in my life, teaching me the strength of simplicity and the beauty of nature's rhythm.

To the one who provided the foundation for my dreams, who ensured I had the space to learn and grow, Akua Bempomaa, your sacrifice and vision gave me the tools I needed to chase the horizon of knowledge and purpose.

Thank you Akua Adadowa, for your unspoken understanding, and for the love with which you have cared for the Eagles, and for giving me the freedom to explore, write, and create.

To my best friend extraordinaire, Meiz Majdoub, for your mentorship and guidance. To David Bennett and Paul Mkandawire, for guiding me on my academic journey.

This book is for all of you—the ones who nurtured me, supported me, and believed in me, without question. Your love, care, and lessons have intertwined with my words, creating the tapestry of this work.

May these poems reflect the beauty and depth of your influence.

---

[2] Akua, signifying Wednesday, is the name given in Akan culture to a girl child based on the day of the week she was born. The day names are:

Sunday: Kwasi (male), Akosua (female)
Monday: Kojo (male), Adwoa (female)
Tuesday: Kwabena (male), Abenaa (female)
Wednesday: Kwaku (male), Akua (female)
Thursday: Yaw (male), Yaa (female)
Friday: Kofi (male), Afua (female)
Saturday: Kwame (male), Ama (female)

Contents

The Ubiquity of Place 2

The Essence of Time 4

Interwoven 6

The Beauty of Life's Light 8

Whispers of Water 10

Water, the Essence of Life 12

A Tale of Injustice 14

Threads of Health and Place 16

Echoes of Mzuzu's Waters 18

Yin Yang of Water 22

Neema! 24

A Realm of Exclusion 26

Chasisi, I Shall Return! 28

Embrace the Natural 32

Wealth and Power 34

Echoes of Environmental Justice 36

Ease The Suffering 38

Where Power Resides 40

Trickster Science 42

Journey of Reconciliation 44

Whispers in Baku 46

The Web of Our Existence 48

Kusi-Appiah

Echoes of Environmental Justice

Painting by Laurence Phiri

The Ubiquity of Place

In every breath, a place is born
A nexus of earth, air, water, and form.
From mountains to oceans, to forests so grand
Each place a tapestry, woven by nature's hand.

In the rustle of leaves, a story's told
Of the land's history, its triumphs and gold.
The scent of blooming flowers, a fragrance so sweet
A sense of place that's rooted, forever unique.

From the frozen tundra to the scorching desert sands
Each place a world unto itself, with its own rhythms and plans.
The urban jungle's steel canyons, to rural landscape's gentle slope
Each place a testament to beauty, diversity, and hope.

The natural world's majesty and humanity's gentle touch
The ubiquity of place, our connection so much.
To the earth that sustains us, to the air that we breathe
A universal sense of place, forever unique in its sheathe.

In this dance between humans and earth
Place is the canvas, where our stories give birth.
A nexus of meaning, where culture, nature, and spirit reign
The ubiquity of place, our place within the empyrean domain.

Ubiquity of Place explores the idea that every breath we take connects us to a unique, ever-changing place. It highlights the diversity and beauty of different landscapes — from mountains to oceans, forests to deserts — and how each place holds its own history, character, and story in time.

The poem reflects on the relationship between humans and the earth, emphasizing how places shape us while we, in turn, shape them. It suggests that while our connection to the world around us is universal, it remains deeply individual, with each place offering a distinct, meaningful experience.

The poem celebrates the interconnectedness of nature, culture, and human life, underscoring the importance of our connection to the planet.

The Essence of Time

Time, a mystery we inhabit, not measure,
A lived experience, not a quantified treasure.
We dwell within its depths, yet try to contain,
A force that flows through us, like a river's refrain.

Durée, a notion born of Bergson's insightful mind,
A plea to acknowledge time's subjective design.
In an age of algorithms and obsessive quantification,
We've forgotten time's essence, its intimate relation.

We've made a formula for everything, it's true,
But in doing so, we've lost sight of time anew.
Its rhythms, its pulses, its ebbs and flows,
The way it lives within us, as our hearts beat and glow.

Time is not just a metric, a unit to behold,
But a lived experience, a story yet untold.
It's the way we feel sun's warm touch on our skin,
The way memories linger, scent of blooming flowers within.

So let us remember, in our quest to measure and know,
The essence of time, as it lives and grows.
For time is more than a concept, a theory to be proved,
But fundamental to our humanity, a mystery that moves.

The Essence of Time challenges the modern obsession with quantifying time, urging us to recognize it as a lived, fluid experience rather than a rigid metric.

Drawing on philosopher Henri Bergson's concept of *durée* [duration of lived time], the poem highlights the way time flows through human existence, shaped by emotions, memories, and nature's rhythms. It contrasts this organic perception of time with society's mechanical, algorithm-driven need for measurement and control, suggesting that in our pursuit of efficiency, we have distanced ourselves from time's deeper essence. This idea connects to environmental justice by emphasizing the disconnection between modern systems and natural rhythms. Just as time has been commodified and quantified, so too has the environment been reduced to resources, productivity, and economic gain rather than being valued for its intrinsic, life-sustaining qualities. Indigenous and marginalized communities, who often live in closer harmony with nature's time, are disproportionately affected by industrialization's disregard for ecological balance.

The poem implicitly critiques this mindset, reminding us that true justice, whether social or environmental, requires a shift from exploitation and control to respect, balance, and lived experience. By embracing time's natural flow, we might also reimagine a world where environmental stewardship is rooted in coexistence rather than conflict.

Interwoven

Within the fabric of earth
We're threads of life, of diverse birth.
The rustling of leaves, a whispered tone
A language shared among beings, made of earthy bone.

The songs of birds, a chorus so grand
Echoing through forests, trees taking their stand.
The buzzing of bees, a hum of delight
As petals unfurl, in the warm sun's light.

In this tapestry of life, we're woven as one
With every living creature, beneath the golden sun.
Our stories intertwine, in a narrative so old
A testament to beauty, forever told.

Interwoven speaks to the deep connection between all living beings and the earth, highlighting how every element of nature — trees, birds, bees, and humans — forms an intricate, unified system. This concept ties into environmental justice issues by illustrating the interconnectedness of life and the importance of preserving the natural world. The poem suggests that when one part of the fabric is harmed, the entire system is affected, a theme that resonates with concerns about environmental degradation, biodiversity loss, and the importance of protecting nature for the well-being of all.

In relation to environmental justice, the poem evokes the idea that humans are not separate from nature but are part of the same ecosystem. It underscores the need for harmonious coexistence and mutual respect among all people, aligning with the core principles of environmental justice, which advocate for equitable access to a healthy environment for all people, especially marginalized communities who often face the brunt of environmental harm.

The term 'interwoven' reflects the holistic approach for which environmental justice advocates, where the health of the environment is intrinsically linked to the health of people and societies, and where collective action is necessary for sustainable change.

The Beauty of Life's Light

In rivers of life our bodies flow,
A vast network of waters, that ebb and flow.
From the source of our soul to the sheen of our skin,
Life-giving force pulsates from within.

Our cells, tiny lakes, drink deep and wide,
Quenching thirst, nourishing, side by side.
Our blood, a stream, carries life's design,
Oxygen, nutrients, and dreams intertwine.

Our muscles like ocean waves, flex and unfold,
As water's lubricating touch makes movement bold.
Our joints, gentle brooks, flow with ease and might,
As water's soothing balm calms the darkness of night.

Yet, in a world of wonder, where water's essence flows,
We've commoditized this gift, locked in repose.
Trading life's elixir for coins as profits sway,
Discarding the wisdom, water's life-giving way.

Let us remember the rivers that flow,
And honor their sacredness as a gift to know.
Let us cherish its life-force, and preserve its might,
In water's flowing essence lies the beauty of life's light.

The Beauty of Life's Light celebrates the vital role of water in sustaining life, both physically and spiritually. It draws parallels between the water within our bodies — flowing through our cells, blood, muscles, and joints — and the streams, rivers and oceans that nourish the earth.

These reflections lament how water, once a sacred and life-giving force, has been commodified and exploited for profit, losing its inherent value.

The poem calls for a return to honoring water as a precious gift, emphasizing that in its flowing essence, we find the true beauty and light of life.

Whispers of Water

In Mzuzu's heart beneath the urban sky's array,
Women weave their silent art,
With water's flow and steadfast heart.

Streams that murmur ancient songs,
Where ancestral spirit belongs,
Purity in every tide,
Sanctuary where hope resides.

Scarce drops in parched domestic veins,
Echoing resilient refrains,
They draw from sources deemed unsure,
Crafting dreams that must endure.

Kachasu's potent, hidden brew,
Born from waters deep and true,
Symbol of both life and night,
Balancing darkness with the light.

Class and gender intertwine,
In the dance at water's sign,
Navigating moral streams,
Fueling clandestine dreams.

Political echoes blend
With ecology's gentle bend,
Feminine strength in every sip,
Guiding through each tightened grip.

Complex ties of earth and soul,
Water's essence makes them whole,
In the city's crowded space,
Women find enduring grace.

Through shortages, fears, and spirits' call,
Women rise and never fall
Where whispers of water gently flow.

Whispers of Water reflects the strength and resilience of women in Mzuzu[3], Malawi, as they navigate the challenges of water scarcity and its cultural significance. It portrays women drawing water from uncertain sources, weaving dreams and hope despite hardships.

The poem highlights the connection between water, gender, and class, showing how women's strength emerges through their roles in society, balancing both light and darkness. Water is portrayed as both a physical necessity and a symbol of life, spirituality, and endurance, linking women's experiences with the broader political and ecological landscape.

The poem is testimonial of women's spirits remaining unbroken through struggle and scarcity, while their stories flow like water in the city.

---

[3] *Mzuzu* is the largest city in northern Malawi and the capital of Mzimba District. It's situated in the Viphya Mountains and is known for its natural beauty, scenic views, and vibrant markets.

Kachasu is a traditional Malawian spirit made from fermented maize (corn) or other grains. It's a strong, homemade brew that's popular in rural areas and is often consumed during social gatherings and celebrations.

Water, the Essence of Life

In a future bright, where wisdom guides our way,
We will shatter the myth, that water's price must pay.
The discourse around this life-giving resource
Will shift from 'economizing' to human right perforce.

We will recognize that water is a gift divine,
Essential for life, not a commodity to confine.
Arguments that infrastructure costs must be borne
Will cede to truth, that water is a human right sworn.

'Water is life' will ring true once more,
Abandon "no money, no water" forevermore.
We'll strive for a world, where every soul can thrive,
With access to clean water, our fundamental right alive.

In this future bright, we will prioritize the earth,
And value water, a treasure of infinite worth.
We'll work together, ensure that all share,
The abundance of water, available everywhere.

Let us envision a world where water flows free,
Where every human has access, grateful and carefree.
Let us strive to make this vision a reality,
For the future of our planet, treat humanity with dignity.

Water, the Essence of Life envisions a future where water is recognized as a fundamental human right, not a commodity to be bought and sold.

The poem critiques the current system that treats water as an economic good, emphasizing that access to clean water should be universal and free. It calls for a shift in mindset, from prioritizing profits and infrastructure costs to valuing water as a life-sustaining resource.

The poem imagines a world where water flows freely for all, and humanity works together to protect this essential gift for future generations.

A Tale of Injustice

In ancient ponds where waters flow,
A tale of injustice has long been known.
A burden placed on women's shoulders strong,
To fetch and carry, the weight of life, all day long.

Who decreed that daughters of the earth
Must bear the weight, of this daily rebirth?
Who decided that women's hands be the ones
To haul buckets beneath the burning sun?

Is it a warped mentality that determines our way?
A twisted logic that says women must pay?
Pay with their time, their energy, their sweat,
The privilege of fetching water, at times under threat.

But the world is awakening to a new dawn's light,
A world where equality will guide our sight.
Where men and boys will stand alongside
And share the burden of this daily tide.

For water is life, and life is for all
Not just for women, for every single soul.
Let us rise, and demand a change,
A world where water's access is plain.

Break free from the shackles of the past,
And forge a new future, equality to last.
For the daughters of the earth, and the sons too,
Will together create a world that's just, pure, and true.

A Tale of Injustice highlights the gender inequality surrounding the collection of water, where women and girls bear the burden of fetching water for their families under harsh and at times threatening conditions.

The poem questions the unjust traditions that place this responsibility solely on females, urging for a shift towards equity. It envisions a future where men and boys share this responsibility by ensuring that access to water is not a burden based on gender.

The poem calls for a world where equity, equality, fairness, and justice reign, and where all people, regardless of gender, can collectively create a better, more balanced future.

Threads of Health and Place

Across Africa's core, crises fester,
Neocolonial chains exploit.
Colonial wounds still endure
Leaving nations strained and poor.

Local elites with hidden aims
Pretend to fight poverty's flames,
But people's voices rise in might
Demanding justice, shedding light.

Grandma Akrasi's wisdom flows,
"Never stop learning," she bestows,
A guiding star in quest of truth
Inspiring minds, aged to youth.

Reclaiming heritage's grace,
Ubuntu embraces our shared space,
Communal knowledge, earthy ties,
Holistic wisdom never dies.

Resist the chains of neocolonial,
Hold leaders true and mutual,
Prioritize the people's due,
Build a world to thrive and renew.

Together, hearts and minds align,
Healing through ties that bind,
A brighter dawn for me and you,
Threads of health and place are true.

Threads of Health and Place explores the intersection of health, place, and social determinants of health, highlighting how our physical well-being is deeply shaped by the environment we live in and the systems that govern us. It emphasizes the importance of understanding how socioeconomic factors, power structures, and community dynamics influence health outcomes.

In relation to environmental justice, the poem calls attention to the ways that place — whether through environmental conditions, socio-political factors, or historical contexts — affects the health of communities, particularly marginalized groups. It advocates for holistic and communal approaches to address these inequalities, suggesting that true healing requires a deep understanding of both the social and environmental factors at play.

The poem champions the importance of empathy, respect, and collective action to address these interconnected issues, aiming to create a more just world where everyone's health and well-being are prioritized.[4]

---

[4] *Ubuntu* is an ancient African philosophy that originates from the Bantu peoples of Southern Africa. Derived from the Zulu and Xhosa languages, ubuntu roughly translates to: "Humanity towards others", "I am because we are", and "A person is a person because of other people." Ubuntu recognizes the interconnectedness and interdependence of all people; it emphasizes the importance of community, mutual respect, empathy, and compassion. In essence, ubuntu is a way of living that acknowledges that our individual humanity is inextricably linked to the humanity of those around us.

Echoes of Mzuzu's Waters

In Mzuzu's urban sprawl
Women stand where waters fall,
Navigating scarcity, enduring pain,
In the dance of loss and gain.

Growth and barriers shape the tide,
Yet non-market threads still guide.
Kinship bonds and cultural streams
Flow through hopes and fractured dreams.

They draw from wells of lore and blood,
Where spirits soar, good dreams flood,
Through labor and *ganyu's* pact,
Vulnerability, strength intact.

Generations pass the flame,
Water's legacy and name,
Sacred waters, pure and true,
Where resilience and culture grew.

Policies must honor ties,
Equitable waters that arise,
Voices echo, strong and right,
Guiding Mzuzu to the light.

Echoes of Mzuzu's Waters highlights the resilience and strength of women in Mzuzu, Malawi, as they navigate the challenges of water scarcity within an urbanized setting. Despite the city's rapid growth and economic barriers, the poem emphasizes the importance of non-market forces — kinship, cultural traditions, and community networks — in shaping their lives.

It reflects on how water, both a physical and symbolic resource, intersects with women's labor, social ties, and the legacy of adversity, particularly through practices like distilling *kachasu* (artisanal alcohol).

The poem calls for equitable policies that recognize these non-market contributions, urging a future where water and culture flow freely for all, guided by shared understanding and resilience.[5]

---

[5] *Ganyu* is a term from Malawi, referring to a system of labor-for-reward or reciprocal labor, where individuals work together to accomplish tasks, often in exchange for food, money, or other forms of compensation. This practice is an important part of Malawian culture and community building.

Kusi-Appiah

Echoes of Environmental Justice

Painting by Laurence Phiri

Yin Yang of Water

Plenty surrounds us, yet scarcity remains,
A paradox of water, where some still feel the pain,
Malawi's Lake Malawi, a treasure so grand,
Sadly its beauty cannot quench the land.

The marginalized masses, with lips parched dry,
Yearn for a drop of potable water, to catch their eye,
But alas, it is a luxury reserved for the few,
A cruel irony in a land of water anew.

Canada's vast expanse of lakes where rivers roam,
Among Indigenous peoples' rights to water is overthrown.
For the sins of colonization stole their land and right
To access clean water, a basic human right.

The yin yang of water, a symbol of balance and harmony,
Is disrupted by injustice, a discordant symphony,
The pool of plenty, a mirage, that taunts and teases,
A reminder of the inequality, that brings diseases.

When will this injustice end, this deprived plight?
When will the marginalized access water, a basic human right?
'I hate injustice' echoes through the land,
Right the wrongs of this water-stained hand.

Let us rise and demand a world where water is free,
For all people, regardless of creed or ethnicity,
Let us break the chains of oppression and might,
And flow like rivers, in a world where justice shines bright.

Yin Yang of Water explores the stark contrast between the abundance of water in some regions and the scarcity faced by marginalized communities. It contrasts the beauty of Lake Malawi, where much of the population lacks access to clean water, with the Indigenous peoples in Canada who, due to the colonial legacy, struggle for their right to clean water.

The poem highlights the injustice of water inequality and the harmful effects of this imbalance, urging for collective action to ensure water as a basic human right for all, regardless of ethnicity or status.

The poem seeks a world where water is freely accessible to everyone, and justice flows like rivers, unimpeded by oppression.

Neema!

A life once bound by fragile fate,
Now soars on eagle's wings, elate.
Sixty orbits of the sun, a milestone rare,
For one with sickle cell, a life beyond compare.

In Ottawa's vibrant tapestry, she shines so bright,
A twin, a trailblazer, in morning's first light.
Her story, woven with threads of resilience and might,
Inspires a generation, to seize the day and take flight.

With every workout, she defies the odds,
Her vibrant spirit a testament to life's gods.
Organic foods, a symphony of nourishment and care,
Holistic harmony echoes through the air.

In the realm of art, her music flows like a stream,
Albums born of passion, a soul's deepest dream.
Family love, a sheltering tree standing through life's storm,
A healthcare system to support and transform.

Her journey, a beacon of hope for those who walk the same,
A shining model of life's potential, unchained and reclaimed.
As we celebrate this milestone achieved with grace,
We honor her spirit, the life she chose to embrace.

Neema! is a tribute to resilience, celebrating a woman who has defied the odds of sickle cell disease for sixty years through a combination of holistic wellness, community support, and access to healthcare.

Her journey highlights the profound impact of place on survival, her ability to thrive in a place with advance medical care and access to organic, nutritious food, contrasts starkly with the reality she might have faced in another place, where healthcare infrastructure and environmental conditions pose significant challenges. This disparity underscores a key aspect of environmental justice: place matters! The quality of air, water, food, and healthcare is not equally distributed across the globe, and those in underprivileged regions often suffer from systemic neglect.

This poem is deeply personal, and it reflects the broader reality that access to life-sustaining resources is shaped by place, privilege, and environmental policies, making her survival a testament to both individual strength and the inequities that define global health and environmental justice.

A Realm of Exclusion

In a world not built for me,
A realm of exclusion, I'm forced to see,
As a citizen of African descent I stand
In a land of settler colonialism, my presence planned.

The streets are narrow, the sidewalks uneven,
The buildings tall, with entrance forbidden
To those like me, with bodies that roam
In a world that's not designed to welcome me home.

The parks are green but not for all,
The trails are winding, forcing some to fall,
The public spaces, a reflection of the past,
A world that's not inclusive, leaving some aghast.

In defiance I rise with a voice that's clear,
Demanding justice for an environment that's dear,
A world built for all, regardless of ability or skin,
A world for everyone to thrive and live within.

The trees sway in the gentle breeze,
A symbol of resilience facing adversity.
The rivers flow, with a voice that's strong,
A reminder of the power of a world, where all can belong.

Let us strive for a world that's just,
Where everyone can live, not forced to adjust,
A world built for all, with accessibility in mind,
A world where all can thrive and leave their mark in time.

For I am not just a citizen of African descent,
I am a human being with a right to be present.
In a world that's built for me, and for all,
A world where everyone can live, without expecting to fall.

A Realm of Exclusion speaks to the exclusion and challenges faced by people of African descent, especially in environments designed without consideration for accessibility.

The poem critiques the physical and societal barriers that prevent full inclusion in public spaces, emphasizing how infrastructure often overlooks the needs of diverse communities. The speaker demands justice, calling for a world that is inclusive and equitable, where everyone — regardless of background or ability — can thrive. It envisions a society where accessibility is a fundamental right, and where no one is forced to adjust or be excluded.

The poem is a powerful vision of a future where all people can fully participate and leave their mark in a world without barriers.

Chasisi, I Shall Return!

Dedicated to my good friend, Chimwemwe Soko

Beneath Malawi's northern stars, my footsteps gently roam
To Chasisi's whispered paths, the ancient spirits' home.
Far from neon gleam and restless urban tide,
In Chasisi, a silent grace and pride reside.

No faucets sing their ceaseless song, no streams adorn the night,
Yet every dawn's embrace renews the village light.
No hum of engine breaks the dawn, no shadows cast by wires,
Just dawn's first breath and twilight's hush, untouched by city fires.

Winding trails through earthen veins where stories intertwine,
Each step a dance on rugged soil where heart and hope align.
No sterile halls to mend the weak, no urgent cries to quell,
But hands entwined in steadfast work beneath a starlit spell.

No vaults of silver dreams to hold, no treasures locked away,
A tapestry of trust and kin, in woven hues of day.
No aisles to wander lost in thought, no glimmer on display,
Just open fields and whispered winds where children laugh and play.

Yet in this plain of seeming void, a hidden wealth does gleam,
The fertile earth, a mother's gift, sustains ones every dream.
The livestock graze on emerald swards, a living ode to earth,
Chickens flit and goats ascend in cycles of rebirth.

Chasisi's souls, a radiant weave, industrous and bright,
Their gratitude like morning dew reflects the soft daylight.
Their smiles, a beacon in the dusk, their laughter pure and free,
A sanctuary of kindred hearts where love flows endlessly.

I pledge to journey back again, with spirit lifted high,
To bathe in Chasisi's warmth again and to embrace the sky.
For in their humble haven a sacred truth unveiled,
That joy and purpose flourish where simpler hearts have sailed.

In **Chasisi, I Shall Return!** the speaker journeys from the neon glow of urban life to the quiet pulse of a Malawian village. Lacking faucets, electric lines, or paved roads, Chasisi appears sparse at first, yet its communal heart beats with gratitude and unity. Livestock graze freely on fertile fields, chickens scuttle among children at play, and neighbors rely on each other rather than on the hum of machines.

This intimate bond with the land echoes the core of environmental justice, for the villagers embody a lifestyle in which every resource is cherished and shared. Without modern infrastructure, they find richness in the kindness that flows between them and in an unbroken relationship with the soil underfoot and the sky above.

The promise to return suggests the speaker's longing to protect and rejoin this grounded simplicity — a reminder that true wealth resides not in possession but in stewardship of the earth and the kinship it fosters.

Kusi-Appiah

Echoes of Environmental Justice

"true wealth resides…
in stewardship
of the earth…"
—Kusi-Appiah

The author in Chasisi. Photos by Mr. Chimwemwe

Embrace the Natural

In a world of plenty, taste buds roam,
Lost in a sea of processed unknowns.
We crave the junk — salty, sweet, and fine,
When we eat real food, call it 'diet divine'.

Isn't it strange, this twisted turned-around tale
That real food's a rarity while junk prevails.
Trading wholesome goodness for manufactured fare,
Our bodies now suffer ailments beyond compare.

Why do we shun the natural, the earthy, the true,
Opting for artificial flavors, that allure and woo?
Is it convenience, or habit, or lack of knowledge and care
That leads us to devour processed junk food as fare?

Savor the joy of eating real food in its prime!
Fruits, vegetables, whole grains, and lean proteins sublime.
Rediscover the pleasure of earth's fare,
And make real food our norm, our standard to bear.

Eating real food is not dieting, it's just right,
A return to nature's rhythm, a celebration and delight!
Let us savor the flavors, the textures, the zest
Of real food, wholesome goodness, that's always the best!

Embrace the Natural critiques modern eating habits, highlighting how processed foods have become the norm while natural, whole foods are increasingly rare.

The poem laments the shift away from wholesome, nourishing food towards artificial, fast food options, driven by convenience, habit, or lack of knowledge. It calls for a return to eating real food — fruits, vegetables, whole grains, and lean proteins — celebrating the health and joy that come from consuming food in its natural state.

The poem encourages a rediscovery of nature's flavors and a rejection of snacks and diet fads in favor of wholesome, everyday nourishment.

Wealth and Power

A truth so stark, yet hidden from sight,
As billionaires speak, with tongues that ignite.
A fire of distraction, a smoke screen so grand,
To divert our attention from the real problems at hand.

They say it is pronouns and woke too,
The real issues facing us in all we do.
But do not be fooled by their clever guise,
For they benefit from status quo compromise.

Their wealth and power built on backs of the poor,
Their privilege and influence forever in store.
They will point to symptoms, but never the disease,
To prevent us seeing systemic inequalities.

Let us not be distracted by their words so bold,
Let's discover root causes of problems we're told.
Follow the money, see where it leads,
To the real issues facing us, born of greed.

It's not about pronouns, or woke, or any other guise,
It's the concentration of wealth and power in their eyes.
It's about the systems that keep us oppressed and poor,
It's about the billionaires who hold us in store.

Wake up, unite, and see the truth glaring,
Let's not be distracted by their words or daring.
Let's fight for a world, that's just, fair and right,
Where all have opportunity to thrive and take flight.

Wealth and Power fiercely critiques the systems of inequality perpetuated by the wealthy elite, who use distraction tactics to deflect attention from the deeper, systemic issues.

The poem underscores the concentration of wealth and power at the expense of marginalized communities, suggesting that the real battle lies in confronting these entrenched structures of oppression, not the superficial debates on cultural issues. This theme is clearly tied to environmental justice, as the same systems that fuel economic injustices also exploit the land and its resources, disproportionately affecting vulnerable populations. By highlighting the need to address root causes instead of distractions, the poem calls for a more equitable distribution of resources, where all individuals, especially those from poorer and historically oppressed communities, can thrive.

The quest for justice, whether social or environmental, is about dismantling the systems that perpetuate both human and ecological harm, to create a world where everyone has a fair chance to flourish.[6]

---

[6] The term "woke" has undergone significant evolution and politicization. Initially, it emerged in African American Vernacular English (AAVE) to describe being aware of and attentive to social justice issues, particularly racism. However, in recent years, the term "woke" has taken on a more complex and politicized meaning.

The politicization of "woke" has led to:
1) Cultural polarization: The term has become a rallying cry for both progressive activism and conservative backlash;
2) Pejorative usage: Some people use "woke" as a pejorative to dismiss or mock individuals or groups perceived as overly focused on social justice or identity politics.

Echoes of Environmental Justice

In whispers of the wind, a tale is told
Of lands laid waste, as futures erode.
The echoes of injustice, a haunting refrain
As earth's cries rise, in vain.

Rivers once pristine now polluted,
Forests felled, trees uprooted.
Ancient songs of mountains, silenced and still
As human greed, their beauty kills.

In city streets, a different tale unfolds
Of communities, their health and futures sold.
Toxic air, a poisonous shroud,
A legacy of neglect, in every crowd.

But amidst the ruin, a resistance grows
A chorus of voices, as justice flows.
From indigenous lands, to urban streets
A global cry, for earth's retreat.

Listen to the echoes of the earth
And heed the warnings of her gentle rebirth.
For in her whispers, we hear our own demise
And in her justice, we will uprise.

Echoes of Environmental Justice laments the ravages of pollution and unchecked exploitation, painting a stark picture of rivers clogged with waste, forests leveled, and city dwellers forced to breathe toxic air.

The poem's final verses sound a note of hope, as marginalized voices and communities, including Indigenous peoples, unite in resistance. This call to heed nature's warnings and strive for a fairer world resonates at the heart of environmental justice, insisting that protecting the planet and uplifting those most affected by environmental harm are inseparable pursuits — and that our own well-being is bound to the health of Earth itself.

Ease The Suffering

In Africa's heart, a crisis unfolds,
A legacy of colonialism, wounds that fester and hold.
Neocolonialism's grip, a restricting chain,
Exploiting resources, leaving nations in pain.

Local elites collude, vested interests at stake,
Pretend to fight poverty, spreading dependence for their own sake.
But people will not be silenced, their voices will rise,
Demanding accountability, a new path to realize.

The future uncertain, as wages stagnate,
The gap between rich and poor, a chasm to navigate.
What can be done to stem this tide,
To ease the suffering, take it in stride?

Resist neocolonialism's restraining grasp,
Hold leaders accountable for our welfare at last.
Let us prioritize people's needs,
And build a brighter future, where all will succeed.

Ease the Suffering addresses the ongoing struggles in Africa, where colonial and neocolonial systems continue to exploit resources and perpetuate inequality. Despite the façade of addressing poverty, local elites often perpetuate dependence for their gain, leaving the people to demand accountability and change.

The poem calls for unity, justice, and the prioritization of universal welfare, urging a shift from oppressive systems towards a more equitable future. This directly relates to environmental justice, as exploitation of natural resources, often for the benefit of a few, mirrors the environmental degradation caused by such systemic inequities. The call to challenge neocolonialism and uphold the rights of the people is not only a plea for social justice but also for environmental sustainability, where communities are empowered to safeguard both their livelihoods and the land they depend on.

The poem echoes the global need for environmental responsibility and healing, ensuring that resources are used equitably and sustainably for the benefit of all.

Where Power Resides

To heal the world's deep wounds and pain,
Look not to those who suffer in vain.
But ask instead, who profits from strife,
Who gains from injustice, and enriches their life?

In the shadows, where power resides,
Lies the root of the problem, where profits abide.
Systems designed to benefit few,
Leave many to suffer, no end in view.

So let us seek truth and expose the facts,
On those who profit from nefarious acts.
Only by confronting the root of this might,
Can we hope to heal, find joy in dawn's light.

Where Power Resides challenges us to look beyond surface-level suffering and ask who truly profits from injustice.

The poem reveals that inequality is not accidental but rather a product of systems designed to concentrate power and wealth in the hands of a few. It calls for critical awareness and collective action, emphasizing that true healing can only come when we expose and dismantle these structures of exploitation. This message directly connects to environmental justice, as the degradation of the planet disproportionately affects marginalized communities while indirectly benefiting powerful corporations and elites. Those who pollute the air, exploit natural resources, and drive climate change often do so for profit, leaving vulnerable populations to bear the burden of toxic waste, deforestation, and water scarcity.

By shining a light on these power structures, the poem urges us to hold accountable those who extract wealth at the expense of people and the planet, and to confront systemic injustices in order to create a more just and sustainable world.

Trickster Science

In realms of power, where truths are spun,
Trickster science weaves, a tapestry begun.
Political ecology, a subtle art,
Exposing power, desires of the heart.

With cunning guile, challenging might,
Dominant narratives, and recurring slight.
It reveals the threads, that weave and bind,
The interests, the power, voices left behind.

In complexity's depths, it finds its way,
Through intricate systems, night and day.
It navigates uncertainty's controlling tide,
And finds the leverage, to shift and glide.

With activist heart, and scholar's eye,
It co-creates knowledge, reaches for the sky.
Amplifying voices, marginalized and worn,
It challenges the status quo, and seeds are born.

For a future just, and a world aright,
Political ecology weaves, day and night.
Trickster science, with a heart so bold,
Shaping the future, a story to unfold.

Trickster Science highlights a field that deftly challenges entrenched power and reveals the unseen forces that shape ecological and social systems.[7]

By weaving together scholarship, activism, and marginalized voices, political ecology exposes how interests and influence intertwine to produce environmental and societal injustices. This 'trickster science' navigates complexity and uncertainty, urging us to question prevailing narratives and seek out the leverage points for real change.

The poem's commitment to inclusive knowledge-making and advocacy ties directly to environmental justice by showing how the health of landscapes and the well-being of communities depend on recognizing and dismantling the inequities hidden within political and economic structures.

.

---

[7] Trickster science is an emerging field that combines indigenous knowledge systems with Western scientific methods to develop innovative solutions for environmental and social challenges

Journey of Reconciliation

A new dawn breaks, a future unfolds,
Where Canadians unite, young and old.
Reconciliation's call, we must heed and share,
A journey of healing, with love and care.

We must move beyond words to actions true,
And practice reconciliation in all we do.
Within ourselves, our families and communities wide,
We will foster respectful relationships, side by side.

In government, churches, workplaces and schools too,
We will strive for understanding, and a spirit anew.
We will listen, learn, and grow, with open heart and mind,
And weave a tapestry of trust, to embrace mankind.

Together we will engage and commit to this noble quest,
Establish and maintain relationships that bring out our best.
Respect, empathy, and kindness will guide our way,
As we build a brighter future, starting today.

In this journey of reconciliation, we will find our strength,
In the diversity of our voices, the unity of breath.
We will rise above challenges, seize opportunities with pride,
Create a Canada wherein all can thrive.

Journey of Reconciliation envisions a future where Canadians of all ages, backgrounds, and beliefs come together to heal and reconcile through respect, understanding, and compassionate action.

The poem calls for a shift from mere words to tangible, everyday efforts to build respectful relationships within families, communities, workplaces, and governmental spaces. It envisions a country where healing and unity are actively fostered, and where kindness and empathy serve as guiding principles in shaping a diverse yet unified nation. The journey of reconciliation, driven by open hearts and minds, seeks to celebrate both collective strength and individual difference, creating a society where all can flourish together.

Relating to environmental justice, the poem highlights key themes of interconnectedness and collective responsibility. Just as the act of reconciliation requires acknowledging past wrongs and actively working toward healing, environmental justice calls for recognizing the harm done to marginalized communities and the Earth, and to take deliberate steps to create a more sustainable and equitable future. The poem's emphasis on inclusivity, shared responsibility, and long-term commitment mirrors the necessity of community-driven efforts in tackling environmental degradation and ensuring all voices are heard in the fight for a just and healthy environment.

The poem champions the ideals of empathy and action, which are essential in both human relationships and our connection to the land.

Whispers in Baku

In November's chill, Baku sees
Thousands gather, hearts in plea.
COP29, a beacon bright,
Where hopes and fears unite to fight.

Will green dreams endure or fade,
As wants eclipse the path we've laid.
Leaders speak of change and care,
But whispers doubt the empty air.

Financial help for lands in need,
Yet promises, pledges lack true speed.
The Anthropocene shadows loom,
As we confront a global doom.

Pause the march, embrace the wise,
Holism, not fame, should rise.
Guardians of earth's sacred lore,
Show us the way to heal and restore.

In Baku's halls, let actions lead,
A greener world is what we need.
Let hearts unite, with nature's song,
To craft a future bold and strong.

Whispers in Baku reflects the urgent hopes and doubts surrounding COP29 [8], where global leaders and delegates gathered to discuss the future of the planet.

The poem expresses concern over whether meaningful action will be taken to address environmental issues, questioning whether promises will lead to real change or remain empty words. It calls for honoring Indigenous wisdom, prioritizing holistic solutions over fleeting fame, and emphasizes the need for concrete actions to heal and restore the Earth.

Ultimately, the poem urges unity and a commitment to a greener, more sustainable future.

---

[8] COP29, an abbreviation for the 29th Conference of the Parties to the United Nations Framework Convention on Climate Change (UNFCCC) held in Baku, Azerbaijan from November 11–22, 2024.

The Web of Our Existence

In the tapestry of our world, intricate and grand,
Threads of fate and time entwine, shaping sea and sand.
Human hues, environmental shades, and places in between,
Interwoven, crafting stories, identities unseen.

Embark on quests profound, to seek and discover
The delicate mosaics that paint our world's vast cover.
Through 'People, Places and Environments', studies refined
To ignite curiosity, insight intertwined.

You'll journey through echoes of our actions on earth,
And how Earth responds, giving life and birth.
The power of place, a mirror reflecting who we are,
Intersections of culture, society, beneath a star.

Engage with stories real and true,
Wisdom to explore, critical thought to do.
Creative sparks, teamwork, navigate the tide
Where global destinies collide.

Join the symphony of voices, shaping understanding's swirl,
Enroll in academic pursuits, let your dreams unfurl.
In this dance of discovery, a truth begins to nurture,
Every thread, every bond, weaves the fabric of our future.

The Web of Our Existence explores the interconnectedness of humans, environments, and places, emphasizing how our actions shape the world in both seen and unseen ways. It invites readers to embark on a journey of discovery, where critical thinking, curiosity, and responsible engagement with the planet open doors to understanding the intricate relationships between society and the natural world.[9]

The poem reveals how culture, environment, and society are shaped by one another, and it suggests that only by acknowledging these links can we truly grasp the consequences of our actions. In relation to environmental injustice, the poem highlights the importance of understanding how environmental harm disproportionately affects marginalized groups, underscoring the need for a holistic approach to justice.

The poem recognizes the mosaic of people, places, and environments, and encourages mindfulness toward sustainable practices, equity, and environmental responsibility.

---

[9] The term "people, places, and environments" (PPE) is often used in educational and geographical contexts to describe the three main domains of study in social studies and geography.

PPE emphasizes the interconnectedness of human societies (people), physical locations (places), and natural surroundings (environments). By considering these three domains together, students can develop a more holistic understanding of the complex relationships between human and natural systems.

The PPE framework provides a contextual structure for learning, helping students to see the relevance and connections between different subjects and real-world issues.

www.ingramcontent.com/pod-product-compliance
Ingram Content Group UK Ltd.
Pitfield, Milton Keynes, MK11 3LW, UK
UKHW050132190625
6471UKWH00008B/146